Birds in America

Steve April

Birds In America
©2016 Steve April
All Rights Reserved. Printed in the U.S.A.

c/o POB 4475
Mountain View, CA 94040-0331

First Printing
ISBN 978-0-9744686-2-4
A Barberry Book

Contents

Birds in America

Preface

Birds fly.

Birds sing.

Emily Dickinson said "hope is the thing with feathers."

They lend such vivacity and abundance, and color to our day.

Considering they have been here millions of years, they are arguably the most successful species on the planet.

Robin

Good egg in spring's exotic billfold,
¼ savior after avalanches, snow,
Messenger of coming, temperate times,
Your orange-red breast matches passion to perfection,
Tweet, tweet sing on our manicured lawns,
Cheerio cheep a pleasing moment in our (busy) day.
A song that carries on the breeze, spreads
A message of hope, and good cheer, and serenity,
Light up our lawns, with your bubbly, charmin' calls,
Forage for earthworms, insects, berries,
In the yards and gardens, upright and potbellied,
Deposit their parts in the mouth of your nestlings,
(Soft, muted 'tseeet' your alarm call),
Rejuvenation at dusk, the song of a robin.

Hermit Thrush

Orange-brown tail raising and lowering when perched,
White eye ring that makes you seem alert,
Your flute like, melodic song echoes through the brake,
Alluring, seductive beauty in the air.
Called American nightingale, and swamp angel,
Star of Whitman's 'When Lilacs Last In the Dooryard
   Bloomed',
Along with the lilac and the northern star,
Why do you raise your tail so suddenly then fall?
You fly south in winter, prefer California, Mexico,
In summer range north country Canada, Alaska,
Start your song with a clear, low note
That spirals upward in a confused, sweet jumble,
Give hope to wayward travelers in bare places,
Bring respite to hearts troubled, or broken.

Yellow-Rumped Warbler

What flash of yellow amid majestic conifers?
Who's tearing at the berries, hopping branch to branch?
Trills in the shadows high up, low and silky.
Spends summers in Canada, way north,
And winters in the south, or Mexico.
Frisky, hardy, flashing your insolent rump,
Calling "cheap, cheep," remonstrating with a peddler?
Engage the forest with your vivid colors behind,
Colorize the deep, dark vernal green,
Your flash of color, never seen by your own eyes.
Bring action to the stately pines,
With your mischievous escapades, romances,
Branches offer you succulent, sweet berries,
Receive scolding drama, color change.

Warbling Vireo

Plain looking, shy little bird,
Your brown coat, and olive-tinged belly engaging,
Beauty being, in force, in the eye of the beholder.
Your meek mien on slender branches,
Give little clue to the riches gushing from your mouth.
From your tiny "5 ½" frame bursts forth song,
A series of unbroken, rich, husky warbles,
That ascend scales, and end on a conclusive high note.
Other vireos may be better looking,
The yellow-throated, the blueheaded vireo,
The white-eyed or the red-eyed vireo,
But your song triumphs over their song,
That are tepid, short, phraselike affairs.
Beware brownheaded cowbirds, nest parasites.

Lark

Soft, murmuring sounds tickle the ear,
Or raised loudly seem to herald morning thrills,
Males hover high over their territories,
And send their songs out on the breeze,
To impress nearby females looking to nest.
Superb camouflage in the farmer's fields,
Where they peck among freshly spread manure.
Only a flock in flight will the red-tailed hawk notice.
With a black facemask, yellow throat, and white belly,
They look substantial aviary citizens,
Denizens that summer in the north, and winter
In the southlands. Like so many brethren,
Fly thousands of miles without a compass,
And find their way home, to their old neighborhood.

Bushtit

Huddle in clusters to share your body heat,
Congregate *en masse*, engaging, social,
Your calls are constant, busy, though not loud,
A thin, soprano, scratchy *zrr zeet*.
Innocuous little "4 ½" tit,
Rounded head and short, black bill
And ones in Mexico have black "bandito" masks.
You look like tiny burglars way up high,
Clumped close to stay warm with your friends.
Males with dark eyes, females with yellow eyes.
Active flockers amid the oak, and juniper,
Enjoy chaparrals, parks, and wooded areas by lakes,
Well-known to mingle, flock with kinglets, warblers,
And mix with wrens and chickadees.

White-Winged Dove

Drinks nectar and rainwater from cactus flowers,
Helps spread pollen among dry-baked cacti,
A dove flyin' exclusively in the southwest USA.
Nevertheless, heads to Mexico in winter.
Loves the woods along the river, brushlands,
Also increasingly found in town and in parks,
White wing patches reveal in flight.
When perched, you see the white wing edge.
Hero or heroine in Stevie Nicks' song,
She conflates their *woo coo woo coo*
With their well known cousin, the mourning dove,
Who coos *ooh ooh wooo woo*.
"Bitches" and males with mild temperaments,
Well appointed symbol for peace and love.

Shrike

Ooh what a pretty bird, and not large,
But its hawkish, hooked bill means business.
Catches small mammals, mice and such,
Also reptiles and other birds. Even so,
The shrike's surprising, musical vocals please.
Are listeners dulled, perhaps lulled by a pretty song?
Last sight for music loving rats, a shrike's masked face.
Otherwise, a bit resembles a mockingbird, in flight,
With a gray belly and white throat.
Wonder why it's been called the butcherbird?
They impale prey on thorns or fence wire,
Let it dry in the sun, like slabs of meat.
In *The Shrike*, a wife's malicious meddling
Lands a Broadway director in a mental hospital.

Scissor-Tailed Flycatcher

Spectacular bird, males' tail long and razor thin.
White head and back, brown undertones,
Who could find a more elegant tweeter,
Imbuing simple branches with a Wow factor.
Bright pinks and orange sides, round out the show.
Courtship flights are like a Hollywood short,
Screamin' male dives and somersaults from 100 feet,
To resume his perch nearby a fluttering, potential
   nest-mate.
After this dangerous courtship stunt,
The male scissortail blandly forages for flies.
Their normal range is mostly Texas,
But they've been spotted far east in Florida.
Miley Cyrus, Taylor Swift, eat your heart out,
What tails hold a candle to the flycatcher?

Baltimore Oriole

Four orioles, Baltimore, orchard, bullocks, hooded,
How about that, a baseball team named after a bird.
The male's orange and black a winsome combination,
The female's a downy yellow and brown.
Graceful and striking like Brooks Robinson,
Third base Hall of Famer. Decisive, Jim Palmer
Pitching strike two. Their connected, slurred whistles
Seem to say, "hey you, hey you, me here singing."
Orchard orioles dive on nectar feeders, and nest in palms.
Baltimore orioles prefer the east coast, like their team.
Cal Ripken, Frank Robinson, Hoyt Wilhelm, Baltimore
Orioles all. Edgar Allen Poe dodged them on the street,
But never penned a tale about the bird
The team's named for, with the tail like quills.

Ring-Necked Duck, Green-Winged Teal

Quack quack quack quack quack,
Children delight to view the floating, vocal gang.
Black head and back, chest bar of white,
There, so sedate, so naturally present,
They bob toy-like, enjoy ripples and swells.
Males utter a high whistle, looking for females,
On small, wooded ponds, mixing with geese and swans.
The green winged teal duck,
With its handsome red head, striped green,
Resembles a Picasso painting miniature.
The greens are fast fliers, and flocks amaze
In mid flight, synchronous coordination.
Greens congregate in shallow, muddy water
Or deep lakes, and perch on fallen logs.

Calliope Hummingbird

The naughty male's crimson throat is striped,
With magenta feathers. So tiny, "3 ¼" small.
Wings vibrate so rapidly, master aerialist,
Descends on barely-open flowers hovering.
Diminutive helicopters, their long bills delicately
    and effectively sip.
Who lends color and grace to a breezy spring day?
They're tea partiers, most colorful guests.
Flit here and there with such joy de vivre.
Enjoy, adapt, sprinkle, delight,
Darling gymnasts of summer, acrobats in spring.
Etiquette style supreme, bright winged being.
Emily's favorite on her garden path,
Seeming to represent a deities' grace note,
Luminous, brilliant, velvet, fiery coat.

House Sparrow

House sparrows are everywhere, all fifty states.
Immigrants from another country, found home here,
To control insects on city streets.
They're successful around humans, they thrive
Where other birds cannot survive.
Females are ho hum gray most of the time,
However, their charms are numerous and varied.
They approach humans, showing no fear.
They skitter playfully down garden paths.
They eat most everything, seeds, suet, insects,
Also breadcrumbs, peanut butter, blueberries.
Chereep, chereep over and over, bubbly, bland.
When a sparrow falls, the heavens note it, says the bible,
Meek and mild forager, brave, audacious.

Red-Breasted Sapsucker

"8 ½", they lean towards heavy weight.
They intimidate at sap wells with beaky thrusts.
The males and females are identical, a very
Rare occurrence in the bird-y kingdom.
They are woodpeckers and enjoy pine woods,
Ratatat tat, ratatat tat, ratatat tat.
They punch a hole to get to the sap, personifying focus,
Or obsession, depending on your point of view.
Their yellow bellied brethren are more common,
Nesting across the northern states in hordes,
And flying south to Texas in the winter.
The yellow bellies are visible only in flight,
And their light tapping contrasts with Big Red,
Noisily drilling and ripping up a tree.

Puffin

If ever a bird resembles a clown,
Or gaudy burble from a circus freak show,
Or alien cutie from another planet,
The puffin fits the bill. Tuxedo
From neck to tail, seems gentlemanly attire.
The large, rainbow bill steals the show.
Oddly, they nest on seashore cliffs, forlorn crags,
On desolate islands, far from peering eyes.
Hunters decimated their population until recently,
Selfishly craving the rainbow hues' good luck charm.
White face, orange feet, a social bird,
Adults feed each other, on steep precipices.
Oddly their call is harsh and guttural,
Easily confused with a drunken neighbor's chainsaw.

House Wren

A rare chocolate covered bird, looks edible.
The diminutive "4 ½" belies a feisty temperament.
Always burbly, with high pitched, liquid tones,
That go jumblin' joyfully, after a harsh starter note.
They scold constantly, *chit chit rrrr-rrrr*.
They intimidate much larger birds,
Who might dare to build their nest too close.
Their nests are slovenly, and odd,
They may nest in a coffee can or old shoe.
Ubiquitous underbird, with character to boot,
They're found in most every state,
Tend to winter in Texas, Georgia, Florida.
Indomitable little wren, the little one may take
The big one, if the little one screams and scolds.

Blue Jay

Shocking blue flashes amid the trees,
Often vents a harsh scolding *jay jaay.*
Also makes rapid whistles, tolling bells,
May imitate a swinging gate with rusty hinges.
 "Blue, navy blue, I'm as blue as I can be,"
With a white underbelly and white wing bands.
Oak trees owe a debt to blue jays,
They store acorns by the score in holes in the ground,
And often jays forget, or don't need to dig them up,
Left to grow into oak trees instead.
Widespread in eastern and central states, in woods,
City parks, and backyards, where they dive on bird
    feeders,
And give scolding alerts to other birds, on occasion,
About diving hawks or swooping owls.

Cuckoo

Koo-kow, koo-kow, koo-kow, koo-kow,
A distinctive call, famously adopted for clocks.
Early in the 1700s, in the Black Forest
Peddlers would carve the charming wooden house
And every hour on the hour, out pops the bird,
To the delight of parents and children alike. Long,
Slender in flight, their specialized stomach
Savors hairy caterpillars no other bird will take.
Black billed or yellow billed, olive above, cream below.
Reddish in flight, striking long tail, yellow bill.
Will drop eggs in, for example, a reed warbler's
Nest, and when the cuckoo hatches it tends
To push out the unhatched eggs. The host continues
Feeding the hatchling, who's *koo-kow, koo-kow*?

Sandpiper

"The shadow of your smile" rings in my ears,
Tender peeps. Riverbank, small stream, sandpipers
    may be there.
Charlie Chaplin teeter-totter, walk along the shore.
In flight, the stiff winged, stutter style's awkward angst.
An aka is *Teeter Peep* due to how it walks,
The least sandpiper named for their peep calls.
Dr. Dre, Kanye, Eminem, fess up.
Your raps could care less about these peeps.
Laughing gulls large enough to swallow them whole,
Pop in suddenly, and dive bomb them.
Beware, little one, with brown back, yellow legs,
No BMW filled with reefer smokin' peeps
Will save you, they are not your brothers,
Nor the faithless, laughing gulls.

Bluebird

In all three families, eastern, western, mountain,
Engaging round head and round body frame the hue.
Oh, plush the soft warble, richly woven song.
Tur, tur, tur-ley, tur-ley. Tur, tur, tur-ley, tur-ley.
When they spot predators they release a contemptuous *couuu!*
Pretty orange breast, always a welcome guest.
The blue bird of happiness, happy to see them.
Funny bird, prefers nesting in open spaces,
Sits on high branches, scouting for moving insects.
Do not need escargot, to have a feast.
They roost en masse on cold nights,
The mountain male a brilliant turquoise blue,
However, lacking the red breast marking their brethren.
Gangs sit on fences en masse a la "the Birds."

Finch

The red male's brilliant attire,
Like he's been dipped in a strawberry smoothie,
So colorful, and such a chipper song, jubilant,
Tweedle-weedle, tweedle-weedle-dee.
 In contrast, the female is tawny, plain.
The male loves to sing, so much so,
He's wont to tip over backward from the strain.
Calling and singing the livelong day to friends and family.
There's house, and gold finches also.
The house's red breast and tawny back
With white spotted belly, a cheerful sign,
They are known to mix with crossbills, grosbeaks.
Cassin's finch call sounds like *giddy up*,
They sport a red crest and pointed, razor bill.

White Pelican

Nine foot wingspan lifting, a sea-spray spectacle.
With a large, yellow-orange bill, *en masse*,
Mothers guard their chicks fiercely in nesting colonies.
For such a big bird, almost never vocalizes,
A few croaking grunts when they are breeding.
They forage in cooperative flocks, hunting herds of fish.
They stalk, on spindle legs, and wait with open bills.
In contrast, the brown pelican dives for its food.
White Pelicans are island breeders, island residers.
Little white face peeks from a brazen, thrusting bill.
O pelicans, your radical style, your appetites,
You resemble twisted, comic pterodactyls, fact check this!
Your pouches hold two gallons of water each,
If lucky, squirming fish are swimming there.

Roadrunner

The famous cartoon makes for a living room celebrity.
The thin, long legs are comic book indeed.
However, this bird's roadkill for coyotes rarely.
A large "22", with a black, crested head
And white spotted body, and enormous tail feathers,
A relentless,voracious predator, nighttime in the desert,
They snatch lizards, snakes, rodents,
Scorpion, tarantula, and tasty insect treats.
Running 15 mph, they'll prey on hummingbirds at
    bird feeders,
Dang them! Strangely their song is dove like,
A series of cooing phrases, love tones,
They do not vocalize "Beep beep beep beep!"
A bird commemorated in song, "Roadrunner" by
    Bo Diddley,
Covered by the Rolling Stones.

Barn Owl

Heart-shaped white face, that makes a Cal Tech
Grad student fall in love. Check out *Wesley the Owl*.
Difficult pets, they attack strangers without warning,
And the way of the owl is not domestication.
They will clear a barn of rats and mice.
The heart-shaped face channels soundwaves to immense
(Hidden) ears. Mostly, they hunt by sense of sound.
The male showers prey gifts on his mate, bloody insists.
Cinnamon brown back, white belly, color coordinated elan.
Little parrot beak belies a large mouth.
Dusk 'til dawn they fly, low to the ground,
Hunting for rats, boll weevils, chickens, assorted varmints.
In the 1800s farmer valued their rodent kills,
A bloody shriek, a barn owl's on the prowl.

Mourning Dove

Coppery breast and head, tawny brown body,
The long, pointed tail, what a tail to tell.
Curvaceous, mild throat and belly, with black spots.
Ah such a mournful, gentle song!
Ooh, coo, ooh coo, ooh, coo, ooh coo.
They perch on air conditioners, terrace rails,
They come to birdfeeders, enjoy suburban lawns,
They fly fast, like a hawk, but the pointed tail
    says "Not."
Hard to confuse with an owl's "who who,"
The tremulous, caressing tone is unique.
Soothes, relaxes humans on the run,
In the midst of our busy day. "My, my," we sigh.
What a gentle, lovely bird, cooing now,
On a balcony railing, outside my window.

Catbird

Elegant, svelte streamer in the branches,
Gray with a black cap, and rusty under patch.
Sounds like a cat with a nasal allergy,
Mew, mew, mew, mew, mew, mew, mew,
Staccato *kak-kak-kak-kak-kak* alarm call.
Catbirds will pierce the nest parasite, tricky cowbird eggs,
And dump them out of the nest, with a victory cry.
They are among the few feathered mimickers,
In thicky, bushy habitat, a vocal skulker,
Maybe the catbird and cat link up in evolutionary terms,
Looks like a cat, with undulating, graceful moves.
The "mew" adds an endearing domestic touch.
Spindly black legs, bloody razor sharp beak though,
Shredding a mouse, in the catbird seat.

Bald Eagle

The bald eagles, you know, are not bald,
They sport a large white head, royal,
A large yellow bill and white tail, with a brown body.
Bald eagles glide gracefully, soar way up high,
They do not rock or teeter like vultures do.
Chattering, high pitched whistles deflate the image,
Sounds like a yapping pup, not a national symbol,
The golden eagles, close brethren, are practically mute.
"What immortal hand or eye dare frame,"
Blake wondered about the tiger. When eagles
Dive hundreds of feet to pick fish off the surface,
That's impressive. "I want to fly like an eagle
To the sea, fly like an eagle let my spirit carry me,"
Their feathers are sacred symbols, Native American lore.

Lark Sparrow, Chipping Sparrow

At "6 ½" among the largest sparrows,
Handsome rufous facial markings, over black neck.
Long, spindly legs, elongated tail,
Sparrow larks are known to sing at night,
The mockingbird's got competition after dark.
Rich, musical blend of whistles call to arms.
They forage in gangs, chirping and pecking busily,
In most central and western states in the summer.
Chipping sparrows are rounder and smaller,
Flat headed with a grayish rump.
Chip chip chip chip chip on and on.
They tend to nest in shrubbery near buildings,
And if given an opportunity to do it, weird brew,
Will line their nest with human hair.

(Black) Vulture

'the walking dead'

When squabbling on or near the nest
Utter guttural hissing sounds, and barks.
They flap their wings, as if straining, between short glides,
Often nest in decaying tree stumps, slovenly undertakers.
Two feet long, with a wingspan five feet,
Feathered gray head, they do not sing,
Vultures feed at open dumpsters in cities,
Roost on powerline towers and dead trees,
Ominous black silhouettes waiting on another's doom.
Barfs predigested roadkill to its nestlings.
Black vultures, though smaller, bully turkey vultures,
And drive them from a nesting site.
No one wants to be their dinner.
Squabbles over the dinner are legendary.

Sharp-Shinned Hawk, Cooper's Hawk

Sharpshinned hawks get mobbed by bluejays,
They scold and scream from adjoining branches,
Terrified and angry. At "13" this hawk is often smaller
Than its prey. They use the element of surprise.
They speed through forest clearings, scattering
Panicked songbirds. "Dirty deeds done dirt cheap."
Likewise, Cooper's hawks prey on other birds.
They spiral high above their prey, and dive.
Victims cannot see the predator, coming out of the sun.
You may call this the law of beak and claw,
In full force, in birdland, when hawks hunt.
"East of Eden they go, in the land of Nod."
They ride thermals, rising areas of hot air,
They drink water from a well.

Brown Thrasher

Whips its head back and forth as it walks,
To thrash leaves and twigs with its curvaceous bill,
To uncover and discover juicy worms or insects.
Engaging rusty back, and spotted white belly,
Farmers formerly set their potato planting
To the thrasher's spring arrival in their fields.
Gives a loud call, like colliding marbles, *chaak*.
Song a repetitive, *digthat planthat, digthat planthat*.
Gangly, exuberant singers with a large repertoire.
Estimated to sing over 1,000 unique, distinct songs,
Including imitating wood thrushes, northern flickers.
Will strike dogs hard enough to draw blood,
When defending its nest. Males and females together
Build an elaborate nest, hard at work up to a week.

Raven

Intelligent, opportunistic, with a long, heavy bill,
Earning a place in folklore, anti-hero in Poe's
    renowned poem,
Perched on the bust of Athena, there croaks "nevermore."
Touches on the haunting realization mayhaps
That the best in love and beauty, stuff of dreams,
In the narrator's life is over, gone forever,
That days of wine and roses are all yesterday,
And shall return "Nevermore," sans exception,
And this happens to us all. Why the raven?
Perhaps the funereal, rich dark feathers,
Or the affable, vaguely forlorn mien,
Or the stately, formal aura, like a good friend's funeral.
The raven flying up against the moon.
The raven rummaging through human garbage.

Woodpecker

Noisy woodpeckers, *rat-a-tat-tat,*
Tree trunk climbers with sharp claws,
And stiff tail feathers, super sharp bill,
Walt Disney started a cartoon, inspired by
Their percussive and obsessive drilling mojo.
Peckers in the morning, peckers in the evening,
They chisel out nest holes, in a favored tree.
They also drum, to announce and defend territory.
The acorn woodpecker's striking clown face
And red crown plumage flash color amid noise.
They store thousands of acorns in holes
Drilled in tree trunks, and maintain these
Hidden granaries communally. Families live in
A large tree cavity, year after year.

Barn Swallow

The graceful barn swallow, a popular bird
Throughout North America, where it swoops
Dramatically over pastures and fields,
The scissor tail either spread or folded.
Gorgeous glossy blue back feathers,
A chestnut forehead and throat.
Sociable, often nest in small colonies.
That glittering cobalt head, what a charmer,
Complemented by a rounded, downy, white belly.
Often cruise only a few inches above ground,
Searching for water. Build their nests
On human structures, barns, sheds, roofs.
They accomplish quick turns and dives,
Often feed on the wing, over 100 feet high.

Crow

In their black robes, they gather above
Like haughty judges. We wonder
What do they have in store for us,
Nailed in the sultry noonday sun?
You may witness them feast
On a dead dog in a country road.
They have good table manners.
On some obscure signal they rise, departing
In a medley of wings and cries,
Their raids complete, and leaving no tracks
In the blue, summer evening.
Legend has it that this once-white bird,
A favorite of the gods, was banished and changed
For talking too much.

Rose-Breasted Grossbeak

At "8" the rose and carmen-breasted sprite
Twitters and soars, colorizing a summer day.
They build flimsy nests, the eggs are often
Visible from the bottom. The male helps incubate
The eggs a few hours a day. They sing to each other,
While trading places. They build the nest together,
Daybreak to sundown. Their bubbly, joyful song
Compares to a robin, but more joyful and operatic,
Drunk on song, or life. They winter in central
And south America. Large bill, big head, they eat
Berries, fruits, seeds, also, foxtail, garden peas,
And tree flowers, bees, ants, and butterflies.
Sadly, due to their good looks and happy song,
They are often snared and sold by bird peddlers.

Cardinal

"Stan the Man" Musial, legendary Hall-of-Famer.
Tony LaRussa, among the winningest managers ever.
Each play for the St. Louis Cardinals,
A baseball team named after a bird.
Fiery red, the northern cardinal flashes color around,
A signature red crest builds to a point.
Bob Dylan said, "only a pawn in their game."
In English class we learn the three major conflicts,
'Man against man, man against nature, man against
    himself."
His reflection in a car window mirror
Causes him to spend hour scolding and clawing,
To repel his double, the imaginary intruder.
To view our own worst fears and enemies,
Dude, take a look in the mirror.

Eastern Kingbird

Talk about personality, this bad-boy bird
Attacks birds much larger, if they draw too near.
Looks like a tough customer, with a black mask
And white below, and heavy-duty bill.
Its crown becomes visible mainly when confronting
Predators, yellow, orange, or red feathers perking up
For crows, redtailed hawks. They diet on large insects,
Which they take back to their perch and swallow whole.
They dive on frogs, and eat them whole also.
The female builds the nest, mostly in the morning,
While the male keeps guard for predators,
Or perhaps rival males. They nest in apple, or haw-
  thorne trees.
Aerial fights occur, where they lock feet together,
And pull out each other's feathers, 'til one flies off.

Acadian Flycatcher

This bird's threat display recalls Dracula.
Spreads its wings and stands straight up,
The way Bella did before notching a victim,
Bill pointed up and waves its body, back and forth,
In a froth and frenzy, like a tiny vampire.
Ghostly buff wing bars, and white eye rings,
A fluttery, high call that sounds like wheezing,
It calls *peet-sah, peet-sah, peet-sah, peet-sah.*
Snatches insects from the undersides of leaves.
Victimized by the thieving cowbirds, which may lay
Eggs in its nest. A very capable flier,
Even able to hover or fly backward, amazing.
Observed to take baths by hitting the water
With its chest, then returning home to shake off.

Magpie

They sit on fenceposts and roadsigns,
Black and white, a bit like a chessboard,
Very long tail trailing behind them.
Steal meat from cougars and foxes, after they kill,
Gather in numbers to feed on carrion.
The only non-mammal species able to recognize
Itself in a mirror test, a study found.
Lewis and Clark reported magpies entering their tents
To steal food, bold connivers. Blackbilled magpies
Mate once for life. The female initiates courtship,
Begging food from the male. Magpies hold "funerals."
When a magpie discovers a dead magpie, there ensues
A raucous riot, and up to forty brethren
Assemble en masse, over the dead bird.

Screech Owl

A small woodland owl, about "8 ½",
Whistlin', tremulous call, rufous (red-brown) coat.
Robin-sized owl with big head, ear tufts,
Long trill or tremulous on one pitch,
Or a quivery whistle, that descends in pitch,
And sounds a bit like a horse whinnying.
Young leave the nest at about 28 days,
Clamor to a tree roost, and are able
To fly about two weeks later.
Preys mostly on small rodents, lizards, frogs,
Large insects, earthworms, snakes, and crayfish.
Mortal enemy also to woodland songbirds.
Does not tend to build its own nest, rather
Uses an old woodpecker hole, or a tree cavity.

Starling

Husky, short-tailed songbird, widespread here,
Struts and frets on lawns, and in parking lots.
Glossy black singer, with yellow bill,
Forms large flocks in winter, often with blackbirds.
Knows how to mimic other songbirds, and with its own
Complex song, interspersed with rattles, click, squeals.
Also whistles *weeeeoooo* and *cheeees*, at odd moments,
Eats insects, berries, and seeds, aggressive "8 ½"
Towards other birds, arguably a big bully,
Exiles native species from their own nests, with harassing
Flurries, pecks, and takes up residence there.
Starlings owe their U.S. debut to the bard,
Introduced to New York's Central park by a wealthy
Shakespeare freak, because mentioned in a play.

Swift

Swifts and hummingbirds share a unique wing,
Their "wrist" and "elbow" joints are very close
To their body, and their wings swivel and gyrate
At the shoulder, aids in pliability and rapid wing beat.
Swifts are clocked at over 100 mph, and may stay airborne
For years. They are indeed swift, sky pilots.
Gather nest material entirely on the wing,
Downy material caught in mid air, gluey spit.
Eat, drink, sleep, mate on the wing,
Cannot walk on the ground, tiny legs
Too weak. They love inaccessible places,
Build their nests behind a waterfall, and fly straight
Through the tumultuous outpouring
To get back home. Most mysterious bird.

Hummingbird

Hummingbirds build minuscule nests
From moss and spider's silk, the outside
May be decorated with lichen for camouflage.
Flight is different from other birds, in a figure-8
Pattern, instead of up-and-down flapping,
Enabling hovering, before pulling out of a flower.
A great deal of energy, fueled by nectar,
They visit up to 1000 flowers a day.
They spread pollen between flowers and help promote
Flower reproduction, with sticky feet and wings.
They go into "torpor" mode on cold nights, a nightly
"Hibernation," enabling them to conserve energy.
A tiny bird, bubbly and joyful. Aerial acrobatics
Come with the territory, being a hummingbird.

Scarlet Tanager

Luminous red plumage in spring, set off
With black wings, a gorgeous combination.
It's the breeding male, vivid in red and black,
Splotchy red and green in late summer in molt.
Breeds in the eastern U.S. in a high leaf canopy.
Eats mostly insects gleaned from leaves, also
Small fruit and berries. Will not meet you at Starbucks.
Frustratingly hard to find, they stay in the canopy
Singing beautiful, liquid tunes. A unique *chic-burrr* call.
Tend their nest in oak, hickory, or hemlock forests.
The nest is usually 45 feet off the ground, with clear
View of the ground and open flyways to other trees.
Parents continue to feed their young, up to
Two weeks after they leave the nest.

Mockingbird

Unmated males sing at night, bestow such a gift,
Lush, liquid tones create a sonic tapestry,
What a symphony, unless a person's trying to sleep,
And these singers sing outside your window.
Also, they weave other bird song into their own,
Along with car horns, car alarms, and such.
Longtailed songbirds, no slouch when it comes to defense,
Will dive bomb neighborhood cats who roam too close
To their nests. Nest in shrubs or trees about 10 feet up.
They were not so long ago, shot and killed down south
For being a nuisance. The day the music died, indeed.
Feisty, charismatic charmer, singing the most
Complex songs in birdland, the edgy mockingbird.
"Crazy ass mockingbirds," call out in song.

Pigeon

Peck their way around city parks, jiggle,
Strut, congregate around humans, who toss crumbs.
Amiable, leisurely, with a *coo coo* call,
The doves are brethren, only smaller.
Eat seeds, fruit, aforementioned bread crumbs,
Also acorns, pine nuts, and tree buds. Like to
Nest on buildings and bridges, may raise
Five or more broods per years, nests incubated
By both parents, about three weeks. They seem everywhere
On a ho hum summer day in the park, gobble crumbs
With a dog's sociability, docile, amiable chubbies,
Ubiquitous city denizens, saved lives in WW2,
Find their way home carrying allied info
About advance enemy positions, back to rooftop coops.

Whip-Poor-Will

Short, wheeling excursions, for flying insects.
Calls its name over and over at night, *whip-poor-will.*
Whip-poor-will, whip-poor-will, whip-poor-will,
Latin name includes 'vociferous', testament
To their amazing call frequency, one call
Per second for over 12 minutes, on occasion.
Resemble an owl flying, with large, binocular eyes
That see in the dark. Fill eastern woodlands
With their mesmerizing chants, they roost on
Low branches, relying on their enigmatic low profile,
Their concealing camouflage. Flash of white
On the outer edge of their tail, as they burst skyward.
A cultural meme, the Hank Williams song, "hear that
Lonesome whip-poor-will, sounds too blue to fly."

Yellow-Headed Blackbird

Yellow-headed blackbirds build their nests over water.
Nestling on occasion fall in, and swim for their lives.
They flock in thousands and forage in fields,
And ranchlands, in the southwest. Each breeding male
Attracts a harem of up to eight females. They cooperate
With terns to mob predators, and sound an alarm.
They are aggressive towards marsh wrens, due to
The wrens territorial pursuits and egg-pilfering.
Males perch on cattails and deliver their song,
Among the most noxious in birdland. Their song
Is compared to the sound of a person throwing up,
Or alternately a rusty, buzzing chainsaw.
They eat grasshoppers, dragonflies, caterpillars, ants,
And spiders, to name a few items on the menu.

Blackpoll Warbler

From baptismal fonts, in rites of passage, they journey,
The tiny birds set off governed by instinct,
Or an intuitive guide, to where land turns to sea,
Through squalls, typhoons, over raging seas, rogue waves,
And they wheel south over the waters in morning,
Or dusk, wherever, thousands strong making the trek,
Storm clouds gather, they wing on, thunder
And lightning rends the air, they wing on.
Half of them won't make it, the three day
Non-stop marathon flight, from New England
To the Caribbean, over rough Atlantic seas.
Over 1,500 miles in three days, and will return
To New England the same route,
When the crocuses bloom in the spring.

Blackpoll Warbler (2)

Why do they fly over the ocean
Rather than go the continental route,
At a more leisurely pace, in safer surroundings?
To accomplish the trip in one fell swoop
Immunizes them from trek predation mishaps,
Less likely to meet with red-tailed hawks and such.
Unlike waterfowl, no rest stops for them.
Weaker birds drop into the water and drown.
So, before they go, fatten up, eat hardy,
Storing fat, often doubling their bulk,
To prepare for the three day marathon,
That they undertake every spring, every winter.
Audacious little songbird, your house of trials,
Your incredible journeys, are they so different from ours?

Mountain Chickadee

Cute little fuzzy black and gray bundle of energy,
Black capped head and throat,
White cheek, gray-black wings, and long tail,
Short bill, calls sounds like
Chickadee, chickadee, chickadee, chickadee,
Little bird with big profile around its nest,
Will lunge forward and hiss like a snake
To scare off a predator. Often forages
In mixed flocks, moves in high trees, like pine
Spruce, and juniper, so often difficult to spot.
Will shell seeds by hammering with their beak,
Nests in crevices and also on the ground, among
    native roots.
They eat tree pests like caterpillars, a chickadee
Was found with over 250 tiny caterpillars in its stomach.

Ruby-Crowned Kinglet

Tiny bird with a unique red patch on top,
Only visible on the top of his head when excited.
Hyperactive, busy, calls *juh-dit-dit, juh-dit-dit*.
Otherwise, a plain bird with a white eye-ring,
And moxie, demonstrated by its song, a rich warble,
That sounds like a much larger songbird.
Famously irritable, they "blow their tops" often,
Around other birds. Sticks to treetops in the northern
Woods in the summer, and winter down south
And in Mexico. Constantly flicking its wings,
Smaller than a wren or a chickadee. Preys on
Spiders, scorpions, wasps, ants and bark beetles.
Their bubbly songs fill the forest with music,
Odd that their little bodies have such power.

Common Redpoll

Vivid red cap and pinkish-hued belly,
Perky, with a short, conical beak
And a truncated, spotted wedge tail.
Perhaps fearful of predators or rivals,
They eat hastily, fill pouches in their special gut
With shelled seeds, and later, in safety,
Regurgitate them, shell them, and eat them.
Song *chit-chit-chit-chit-chewee*, and call,
A la David Bowie, *ch-ch-ch-ch-chweee*.
Have an enviable, special capability to survive cold
Temperatures, called "polar bear" among songbirds,
Extra food stored in their pouch
Is digested nocturnally, keeping them warm, next
    morning
Forages with goldfinches and siskins.

Prothonotary Warbler

Darling yellow-headed, yellow-bellied bird,
With grayish-black wings and a wedge tail,
The warbler is named for its golden hood,
Akin to ceremonial garb worn by the notary officer
In the Roman Catholic church.
Mostly residing in the central and eastern states,
Tends to nest in swamps, and wet lowlands,
Sings *sweet sweet sweet sweet sweet.*
Will sing from the treetops but both
Sexes drop from the canopy, and forage low.
Nests in tree cavities, or trees standing in water.
"5" radiance among the dense undergrowth and swamp,
Creating its own unique, woodsy tones.
Curious, named for a church official, amen.

Ovenbird

Builds a domed nest on the forest floor,
Hence its name. Males and females
Look alike and keep their coloration throughout
The year. *Tea-shur, tea-shur, tea-shur, tea-shur,*
An invitation to a tea party in the woods?
Male sings a nighttime flight song above the treetops,
In spring and summer, then drops down
Among the trees. The elaborate, oval nest
Vulnerable to snakes, bears, cougars, or being disinterred
By rains, often survives, under heavy fern cover.
They walk and forage with their tail pointed up,
Tawny brown with a black streaked forehead,
Leopardy, speckly belly, and thin, sharp beak.
Earth colored camouflage, signature oval "oven" nest.

Tufted Titmouse

What a pristine, protectable little bird,
Born into the wild for thousands of years,
And somehow making a living, making its way.
Very large black eyes on a pale face,
Give this cute bird a dramatic, Broadway look.
Their blueish crown tuft stands up on edge.
They look friendly and approachable, larger
Than chickadees they mix with. They sing,
Peet peet peet peet peet, in the mood for coffee?
Also, a medley of tweety, whistled calls.
And a harsh chickadee-like scold when irritated.
They will steal hair from humans and pets
To line their nest. Will often choose old woodpecker
Holes, they adorn with twigs, leaves, hair.

Yellow Warbler

Almost entirely yellow, charming songbird.
A few red streaks on the male's breast.
Song *tweet tweet tweet tweet tweet.*
Truth in advertising on this one.
Big, dark eyes on a plain, yellow face,
Loves willow trees, especially near water.
North American summers, tropical winters.
These warblers build elaborate nests
Often four "stories", with eggs laid
On each floor. The brown headed cowbird
Drops eggs off there, and if detected,
The mother destroys the old nest, relocates the eggs,
And builds a new one on top, thwarting the invader.
Question, are they rid of the intermeddler's eggs?

Golden-Crowned Kinglet

Golden crowned kinglets can hover underneath
Branches to snap insects off the foliage underside.
Nesting in the north, orange-crowned males,
Yellow crowned females. Song is a thin series of
Notes rising in tone, that top-jumbles and falls
Back to scale. Call is *seet seet seet seet seet.*
To catch insects it flicks its wings back and forth
Hoping to startle an insect into moving. Spend
Their time high up in spruce or fir trees.
Bright yellow crown stripe, bordered in black
Hence their name, a tiny, stocky songbird
With olive green wings. Golden crowned,
Ruby crowned, oh the profusion, oh the abundance,
Brethren in flight, remaining, flourishing.

Anna's Hummingbird

Males' bright red crown unique among hummers.
Also, a ruby throat that glitters, a tawny spotted belly.
A vocal hummingbird, articulating chatter-y buzzes,
And raspy notes, as if with laryngitis.
Dips in gently on nectar producing flowers, hovers
With long, soft sips. Ah! The delicacy and strength
Behind such seemingly effortless moves.
No heavier than a ping pong ball, their aerodynamic
Acrobatics are the envy of ballet dancers.
They cannot help but be compared to jewels.
For courtship displays, the males climb one hundred
Feet in the air and dive, making an explosive pop
With their tail feathers. A bright, kinetic blur
Among the flowers they zip around.

Elegant Tern

Thin orange bill, trim black crest,
Kii-riicci, kii-riicci, kii-riicci, kii-riicci,
Streamlined profile, hence the name,
Compared to the Royal Tern.
Anchovies, anchovies, anchovies,
They love em, they want em, they need em,
When anchovies are plentiful these terns do well.
Only in Mexico and California, a relatively rare bird.
Plunge-dives for fish, and the fish offering
Male to female is part of the courtship display.
Flatfooted on two large black feet, on shore,
Rides the thermals, high over the seaspray,
Underparts often with a pink blush,
Their high winding trillish cries adorn the sea.

Laughing Gull

A slender gull with a long, dark bill,
And a bon vivant flying style,
Calls *Ahhh! Ahhh!* or *Ah-ah-ah-ah-ah*,
Sounds like a person laughing loudly.
They will harass weary terns to force them to drop
Their catch. Also harass larger birds, pelicans
And ospreys, easier to get a meal this way
Than to plunge and dive into the freezing waters
Hours on end, diving perhaps vainly into the sea
For fish, and wasting precious energy.
Wheel over beaches with aggressive calls,
Hang out on beaches, docks, and parking lots
Cruising for handouts, or broadly foraging for
Snails, crabs, fish, squid, and berries.

Sharp-tail Duck

Streamlined, riven, catapulting out of the brake,
Or up from a freshwater pond, quick to flush,
Long swanlike necks and tails, elegant
Symmetries, chocolate brown head,
White neck and breast, and belly,
Females are almondy marshmallow.
Females give a *quack quack quack quack quack*
A la Donald Duck, while the males give a high pitched
Toot toot toot toot toot, this entertaining bird
Oh so sleek and svelte in flight, with a sharp long tail,
Eats snails, shell fish, insects, seeds,
Does not dive for fish, rather dabbles on shore,
Filtering food, water pouring through its beak.
"Every girl crazy about a sharp tail duck."

Swan

Little swan with an orange bill
What secrets you hold, in your classic S-shaped neck,
　your bill pointing down.
No "fearful summetry," but moving symmetry.
Floating, buoyed, ready to launch, or simply
Calmly, with unruffled feathers, followed by your
Hatchling, regal, foraging on a lake.
You float on a calm body of water like you belong
There. A pair of mute swans on a park lake,
A symbol of love, devotion, togetherness,
Though harass other birds who intrude
On the pond, aggressive towards an interloper.
"Endless stream that flows to you,
All the tides know what to do,
Little swan, gentle one," sings Salon Recliner.

Western Bluebird

Charming combo blue and orange,
Blue on the head, throat, wingbar,
Tawny orange on neck and breast, with a
Gray underbelly. Female in contrast is
Brown with grayish markings across the throat.
Ty chai, ty chai, ty chai, ty chai
This pretty bird may roost communally on cold nights,
Also, gather in huge flocks, raid juniper berries,
In summer common in Washington, Oregon,
Winters in the southwest and Mexico.
Call note is a scolding *shaq shaq*.
Perches on fences in meadows, and flutters down
To pluck insects off the grass.
Also, flutters among the branches picking berries.

Canyon Wren

A small bird with a large beak and fanned tail,
That creeps along jumbled rocks, along steep cliff walls,
And perches on an enormous boulder, to pour out
A lush, musical song. Russet brown body,
Liquid tones, *tee tee tyew tyew tyew,*
Fills the canyon and cliff faces with song, and echoes,
"This land is your land, this land is my land."
Tiny tike of a bird, that sings lustily, heartily,
Long bill probes for worms, beetles, spiders,
And insects, in tiny cracks between crevices, rocks.
Nest is usually in a hole or crevice
On a rocky cliff. Also stone buildings, abandoned
Sheds. Males defend their nest territory
By singing. Both parents feed their nestlings.

Vermilion Flycatcher

Flaming red crown, throat and breast,
Contrasts with downy brown wings, brown eyemask,
Song *pip pipit zreee, pip pipit zreee,*
They wag and flair their tails on their perch,
Found near open water, streams, and ponds.
In courtship, the male fluffs and puffs his red feathers,
While fluttering and singing, swirling and diving,
Then swoops back to his perch, before starting anew.
Look at that, how he wings through the air,
With the greatest of ease, so light
And quick, quickness at the heart of life,
A rising pulse, a wing flash, they are gone.
Over millions of years, an architecture with jewel
Precision, a spontaneous, expansive free bird.

Belted Kingfisher

Almost comic-looking bird, with unruly,
Disheveled crest, and Pinocchio bill,
May look like a truant schoolboy, or little rascal,
But makes wheeling turns and deep dives underwater
To spear fish with the outrageous proboscis.
Blue crest, gray breast, ardent diggers,
They burrow in sandy banks and build nests
To raise their fledglings. Jerky, irregular
Wingbeats add a clown touch, even at great distances.
May give a rattling call hovering over water,
Before nailing a spectacular, plunging dive.
Bones, scales are expelled later as pellets.
In courtship display, the male brings the fish
To his mate, and attentively feeds her the fish.

California Gull

Ubiquitous California bird that surprisingly
Winters in Utah and central Canada.
Nests on inland lakes and marshes, and forages,
In farm fields, dumps, parks, by and in lakes,
Often resting on docks, beaches, and in parks.
White face and breast, yellow beak, gray wings,
Black tail tip. Varied diet including fish, eggs,
Carrion, insects. Parents feed young by regurgitation,
For about 45 days. They hover and dip to snag prey
On water, or land, with incessant shrill cries.
The story is told, the California gulls
Saved the Mormon settlers' proverbial assets, in 1848
When the gulls decimated grasshopper hordes
Devouring crops, a welcome king harvest came that year.

Red Crossbill

The males' distinctive red crown and breast,
In combo with their strong scissor-y crossed beak,
A bit like a hangnail, gives them a unique,
Colorful patina. They use that strange bill
To leverage seeds out of pinecones, also spruce,
And fir trees. They often hang upside down
Under a pinecone, digging with their bill.
Nests tend to be between 10 and 40 feet up
In a pine tree. In courtship the male performs
Wheeling dives, and may feed the female.
Both parents feed nestlings, young are fed
Regurgitated seeds. Song *twit twit twit twit twit*,
And their call note is *klip klip klip*. Varieties
Abound, smaller-billed feed on smaller pinecones.

Painted Bunting

Not a baseball term, perhaps the most vividly
Colorful bird in the country. Electric blue head
And neck, green shoulders, red underbelly
And breast. Also red eyes, and a white beak.
The female's brownish with a yellow throat
And lime-green wings. Nature bestowed so
Many gaudy, festive hues, that in the tropics,
Where they winter, fowlers trap them and sell
Them as pet birds. Sweet warbling song,
Their call in contrast is a sharp, mechanical *vit*.
Females care for the young exclusively, however
After they leave the nest the male may feed them,
If the female begins a second hatching. Secretive,
And sings from a perch high, high in the canopy.

Lincoln's Sparrow

A warm, chocolate-y breast, with leoapardy
Black spots, and a white throat, yield a charming
Patina, to this little songbird, not named for Abe,
But Thomas Lincoln, Audubon's friend who
Accompanied him on a birding trip in 1833.
A pretty jumble of phrases rises in pitch
And volume, *bree zee bree zee bree zee.*
Nests in thickets of willow and alder,
Shy and secretive around its nest.
Forages while hopping on the ground, around
Dense foliage, eats spiders, caterpillars, beetles,
Moths, millipedes. The busy female builds her nest on
The ground, under a lump of grass, or dense shrubbery.
If approached closely, she will scurry like a rodent.

Trumpeter Swan

The all-white, largest swan, a hornlike tooting
Gives the bird its name. Strident, long notes
Sound like a trumpet. Trumpeter swans pair for life,
And both raise their young. They inhabit lakes and ponds
In Washington state, uncommon in other states.
Largest waterfowl in America, and among the heaviest
Flying birds, they nearly went extinct, due to habitat
Destruction, but conservation efforts and protected
Status, helps bring them back. Young are not capable
Fliers until three or four months after hatching.
Take food from underwater or on the surface.
To dive, they upend with tail in the air, and neck
Extending directly down, for roots of aquatic plants,
Sedges, and rushes. Young swim at a day old.

Indigo Bunting

Electric blue adult male so striking,
So charmin'. The females are brown all year.
Males sing a raucous, engaging song with paired notes
Descending in tone *why why where where out out.*
Call notes are splat and *bzt,* sounds like an electric shock.
They flick their tails out to the side.
Tricks with stars *fx* in a planetarium,
With subject buntings, shows they are guided
By stars during migration. Sing along woodsy edges
In the central and eastern states. Diet on
Insects, spiders, seeds, berries. Young leave
Nest nine to fourteen days after hatching.
Forage alone in summer, in flocks
In winter, the females do most of the work.

Great Gray Owl

Vincent Price would have a field day
With this illustrious omen, perched
Outside our window. Longing for nocturnal
Mysteries, apparitions, haunts, visitations,
Here's your bird. Dark round face
And piercing yellow eyes. Little white chin smears.
Elegantly shaped head and torso streamlined
For predatory hunts. Built-in sonar captures prey
By sound mainly, hears rodents moving below
The surface of the snow, and swoops on them,
Talons outstretched. Male offers prey items
To a mate, presents to her insistently.
Hoo hoo hoo hoo. Stoic mysterioso, winging
Through the night woods, on spectral errands.

Summer Tanager

Aka *Bee bird*, due to bees and wasps
Are on the menu. Utilizes its long, sturdy bill
For snagging and gobbling them, sans annoying
Stingers in the mouth. The male is bright red,
Flashing the wings, in breeding season, with a long tail
And black eyes, the female also colorful, yel-
   low-throated,
Green-winged, with an orange crown.
The strong-toothed bill is inured
To the sting of the yellow jacket, and pesky wasp.
They reside in oak and pine woods generally,
Call *party puck puck party puck puck party puck puck.*
Fly through the air, giving vent to liquid tones
Keats himself would have envied, on the wing,
Before raiding a hornets' nest, for a tasty lunch.

White-throated Swift

White throated swifts may mate
In flight, love on the wing.
Male and female meet high up above the canopies,
Tumble, somersault, perform acrobatic feats,
Before resuming their normal flight patterns.
Call *jes jes jes jes jes jes jes.*
The fastest flier in birdland,
Tend to roost on remote mountain crags,
In inaccessible niches, on a mountain wall.
"6 ½', forages in flocks, flying rapidly
Chitter chattering and sputtering the day away.
Level flight speed clocked at over 100 mph.
Their nest made of feathers, weeds, glued together
To the wall of a sea cliff crevice with their saliva.

Blue-Gray Gnatcatcher

Males with blueish wings, and very long tail
And white eye rings on small faces,
Females with dusky, brownish wings,
Constantly fluttering around, foraging
For gnats and other small insects, snatches
Them out of the air. Call is a mewing
Chee chee chee chee chee. Song a
Confused jumble of high notes, mixed with
Warbles and staccato whistles, they appear
Where insects are active, a spring messenger
A la the robin, very vocal and active bird,
Regularly calling while chasing after gnats and flies,
And picks them off expertly in flight. A tiny
Songbird weighing only about 6 grams.

Brown-Headed Nuthatch

Utilizes wood chips to pry bark,
To access crawling critters,
Spiders, caterpillars, moths, insect eggs,
Very few birds employ tools like that.
Diminutive "4", brown-capped birds, with
White throats, gray underbellies.
Queet queet queet queet queet queet queet queet.
Populates southern, eastern, and central states.
Forages trunks and large limb'd pine trees.
Builds nests in a dead tree. Both sexes help build
The nest, and a "helper" is often observed,
A second male, who brings food to the female
On the nest and young after they hatch. Could
The second male be a sibling? Who knows?

Snow Bunting

Handles extreme cold, up to -60 below zero.
Arctic virtuoso digs into the snow for shelter
In the tundra. In the breeding season there,
Wonderfully white on head and breast,
With black back, bill, feet. The proverbial "snowbird."
Musical warble *tew tew tew tew tew.*
Down south in the states for winter, they sport
Rusty coats, white wings, and black wingtips,
And mix with larks and longspurs. They tend
To beaches, and farm fields, with freshly spread
Manure. Nests are built in crevices on mountainsides.
Colloquially known as "snowflake." During
The last Ice Age, snow buntings were
Widespread throughout the European continent.

Purple Martin

Wheeling high above a nest site,
The male sings a liquid chorus
Warbling *teer teer wew here teer teer*
To entice potential mates into his kingdom.
The largest swallow, the male's glossy blue body
In direct sunlight, glistens purple.
They fly smoothly, and have forked tails.
Swallows are among the fastest fliers
In Birdland, and swoop, dip and pivot,
Gleefully, gracefully, and migrate long distances
With ease. Native Americans centuries ago
Would build them hollowed-out gourds
On poles, to entice them to nest, and martins
Helped the village reducing wasps and flies.

Chestnut-Backed Chickadee

The most colorful chickadee,
Rusty breast and belly, white throat,
Black crown, white-gray fanning tail,
Song a series of rapid, thin chirps.
Chirp chirp chirp chirp chirp,
Also *chickachicadee dee dee,*
Calls psst cheerio psst cheerio,
Unlike its brethren the mountain chickadee
Who calls *chickachicadee dee dee* exclusively,
From where the bird derives its name.
Prefers willows, oaks, pine woods, and redwoods,
The black crown gives a "bandito" touch
To this feisty "4" bird, with glittering black eyes.
Often pairs remain together the whole year.

Black Skimmer

Rare bird, only seen on Florida's southern tip,
Thrillingly skims the water, their unique hunting skill,
A long red bill, a la Cyrano de Bergerac
Plows lightly through the water. Feels for food,
Rather than sees the tasty fish below the surface.
If the lower mandible feels a fish, wham the upper
Snaps shut. They vocalize with a high-pitched *erff, erff.*
Large "16" bird, with splendiferous black
And white wings, masked face, and long tail,
With its exquisite balance cruises perilously close
To crashing at 30 mph or so, into the drink.
What a strange, uneven beak. A face a mother
Would find hard to love. But oh so dapper,
Tilling the water, and cruisin' the coastlines.

Violet Green Swallow

Expert fliers, with glimmering, glittery green
On crown and upper chest, wide they range,
And swoop after insects far above the other birds.
Che chip che chip che chip che chip che chip.
Fly high over mountain forests and forbidding canyons,
Nest in cliff crevices on rugged terrain.
Nest is built by both parents, made of grass, twigs,
Lined with feathers. Incubation is by the female
15 to 18 days. Both parents feed nestlings,
But females more-so. Young leave the nest
About 24 days after hatching. Eat wasps,
Bees, beetles, moths, flies. Iridescent, oh iridescent
Little being, soaring so high, faster than a locomotive.
Bright vivid being dip and pivot, above the human.

Sanderling

Plump, pale shorebirds scamper to and fro
Timing their dashes to the waves' rhythm,
Pursing and probing for exposed sand crabs,
Then run away as the next wave rolls in.
In the Arctic May to August, their breeding colors
Are red-orange with leopard-y spots,
The rest of the year the males sport white head and belly,
With brown plumage. They peck the shore hunting
For morsels, in groups, mostly on the west coast.
When flying they shrilly cry *kip kip kip kip kip.*
In breeding season, males perform low-flight display,
Fluttering and gliding, to a harsh cracking song.
On ground, males ruffle up their feathers, and run up
To females, heads scrunched on their shoulders.

Black-Necked Stilt

Pink, pencil thin legs seem so delicate,
Their crazy-long razor-sharp bill pierces
The water, hunting for fish. Black on top,
White below, with a black crown and big
White eye-rings. When annoyed cries
Kleep kleep kleep kleep kleep kleep kleep.
Needle-like, pincer bill plucks prey jauntily
Out of the water, into the air, maybe tossing,
For a brief moment, then down the hatch.
Parties in marshes, and mudflats, snatching up
Crustaceans, and also insects. Surprisingly
They tend to nest on sunbaked ground, in the open,
Such as salt flats, by shallow lakes. Also,
Plunges head into water to take shrimp, crayfish.

Cedar Waxwing

They pass a wild cherry in a bonding ritual,
And also between flock members,
That looks like they are smooching.
They vocalize constantly *sree sree sree sree sree*.
They will flock and gather wherever
Berry crops are in abundance. They are
Occasionally found reeling in circles,
On the ground, appearing drunk
And unable to fly, after eating fermented berries
In large quantities. Will drink oozing sap.
A warm brown bird, with red, waxy wingtips,
Depending on the season. May hover briefly
While plucking berries or taking insects from foliage,
And flutter the branches while they feast.

Wood Duck

A rainbow of colors, the breeding male,
One does a double take. Looks like
A Norman Rockwell illustration, so vivid and engaging.
Longer tailed than most ducks,
The female whistles 'a week a week.'
Ducklings leap from the nest day one
Out of the egg, and seem to float
On downy fluff, to a soft landing.
Odd ducks, they roost, and nest in trees,
Near swamps, rivers, marshes, widespread.
Tend to fish by dabbling at the surface
Rather than diving headfirst into the water.
Fast, strong fliers frequently call in flight,
Or whistle, *oh oh oh oh oh oh oh.*

Mallard

Green head, yellow bill,
The most familiar U.S. duck, females give a
Quack quack quack quack, from Donald Duck fame,
The males go *queep queep queep queep.*
Newborn ducklings imprint on the mother,
And will follow her wherever she goes,
Famously crossing a busy highway, full of commuters.
Strong fliers, clocked at speeds up to 60 mph.
Among the most abundant ducks in the world,
Young are tended by females, and feed themselves
For about 60 days, then fly away,
Forage by dabbling in the water, not diving,
Grabbing for aquatic roots, small fish.
When fall comes, they fly south.

Ruby-throated Hummingbird

A male ruby-throated flashes a red throat
In front of a perched, attentive female in
A courtship display. The pair,
With glittery, green back and wings,
Exchange high-pitched twitters frequently.
Their wings hum, hence their name.
They are often mistaken for large insects,
A sphinx moth, for example, so tiny
And quick they are, especially the young ones.
They buzz the flowers, sipping nectar incessantly,
They zip around, busy fliers, about their work.
They weigh less than a dime each but
Their wings flap up to 60 beats per second.
They may migrate 400 miles in one day.

Yellow-breasted Chat

Freaks out in a courtship display,
Calls loudly and flaps his wings frantically,
A death-defying, vertiginous plunge seems imminent.
Large head, muscular little chest, thick black bill,
And a long tail. They vocalize constantly, their
    crazy talk,
Erp! Erp! Erp! Woo woo woo! Wonk Wonk!,
Hence their name. They make sympathetic chucks,
Followed by guttural, scalding ejaculations (accusations).
The yellow throat and breast are unique.
They have white eyerings, aka "spectacles."
They sing raucously under a full moon,
Serenading, usually from the cover of deep woods.
Breed in brier patches, willow thickets, nest in tangled vines,
Hold food by one foot while they feed.

Piping Plover

The hatchlings are able to run and peck
And eat their first meal out of the egg
On day one, under their parents'
Protective gaze. Though the female often leaves
The young after a few days, or leaves
The male to care for, and supervise them.
Their courtship displays are quirky and memorable.
Males approach females on the ground,
And stamp their feet in staccato fashion,
While high-stepping in circles around them.
In the air, the male calls incessantly and slows
His wingbeat over her head. A busy
Shore bird with a pale face, and orange bill,
They nest on flats near lakes or rivers,
An endangered sub-species, chunky pipers.

Pine Siskin

Streaky black on brown plumage, and whitish breast,
With a fine-tipped bill, they flash yellow wings
In flight, and are often mistaken for goldfinches.
Indeed, they flock *en masse* and forage
With goldfinches. The male is observed
To feed the female in a courtship display,
And when nesting. They are widespread
And present in all 50 states. They drop and settle on
Fields of thistles or wild sunflowers, where they cleave
To the dried flower heads, eating seeds.
In winter they move south in big numbers, with the
    finches,
And forage upside down in trees and shrubs,
To reach seeds. Nests are usually well-hidden
In pine trees about 30 feet in the canopy.

Green Jay

Lime-green back, violet-hooded crown,
Black throat, yellow belly, this colorful jay
Only populous in southern Texas and Mexico.
Calls *shack shack shack shack shack.*
Raucous, squawking, noisesome, querulous,
May wake you in the morning tapping on your window,
Trying to crack open a nut against the pane.
Ah morning! A variety of rattling calls,
Also including *shink shink shink shink shink.*
Forages by moving actively through trees and shrubs,
Scanning the foliage for food. Drops to the ground for nuts,
And flies out to catch insects in mid-air.
Young leave nest about 20 days after hatching,
And the following nesting season, are evicted.

Mountain Bluebird

Turquoise blue male resembles a wind-up toy,
Glistening crown, black wing bars, gray breast.
May nest in cliff holes or muddy banks, if tree
Hollows are hard to come by. Among the prettiest
Birds in the western states. Hovers in open fields
Then pounces to the ground to seize its prey.
Both parents feed the nestlings. Also, lies in wait
On a rock or low branches, and snags insects.
Eats juniper berries in winter, essential for diet.
The female selects the nest site, usually a
Loose cup of twigs, rootlets, pine needles, stems,
Often accoutered with animal hair or feathers.
Young leave the nest after about 20 days,
And are fed by the parents an additional three weeks.

Cowbird

Sparrow, warblers, flycatchers, vireos, are known to
Raise the cowbird hatchling. The hatchling dumps
Native eggs from the nest, instinctively. The host
Parent often remains ignorant of the switch (duh!),
And continues feeding the usurper for ten days or so.
Sturdy bird with greenish gloss, and dark brown hoodie,
The male's courtship song is squeaky, gurgling notes.
Female grayish brown, with scallop underparts,
She lurks and glides over grasslands, among trees,
Looking for a nest to house her eggs, and after
Doing so, flies away, trusting to childcare.
Ecological bad news, especially for smaller songbirds,
But have gotten away with it, like a blind spot,
In nature's vision, or a mole on her skin.

Golden Eagle

"O beautiful for spacious skies, for amber
Waves of grain, for purple mountains majesty…"
Into the brazen, bronzed mountain air
Ejecting off some desolate crag, in the northwest,
Nestlings crying softly, awfully early morning,
To feed their hungry little mouths, and their own,
Off they soar, about their bloody work. They ride
The thermals. On the hunt, may perch on
A telephone pole, ready to pounce on an unwary
Rabbit. They will kill prey as large as small deer.
Seize them with steely talons, carry them off to the nest.
Golden crown and neck feathers, magnificent
Seven foot wingspan, piercing eyes, sharp beak,
May reach speeds up to 150 mph on an attack dive.

Notes

*Sources include National Geographic Backyard Birds,
Smithsonian Migratory Bird Center, All About Birds,
Field Guide To The Birds, Beautiful Birds, Fastest Things
On Wings, Bringing Nature Home, The Warbler Guide,
The New Birder's Guide, Wesley The Owl.*